There is SO1

t

this P

CW00820322

From Creative Chef Postcards - © 2016 Jasper Udink ten Cate and BIS Publishers - www.creativechef.nl - www.bispublishers.com

Wanna play?

This is actually
ketchup art!

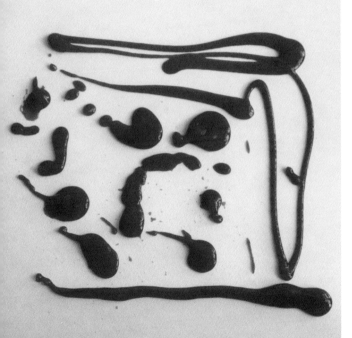

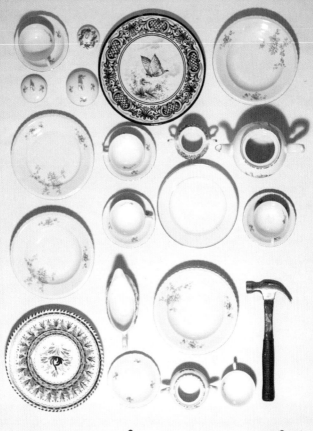

Let's break stuff

Make food
not war

creative chef presents
CAMOU
FLAGE
SALAD

Starring: Romaine lettuce, Shiso Purple, Egg, Tasty Tom Tomatoe, Cucumber, Edible Flowers, Black Olives. **Dressing:** Vinegar, Salt, Honey, Mustard & Olive Oil
Based on the poster of Full Metal Jacket. Graphic design: Timo Venhuis. **Foto:** Rogier Boogaard.
Concept and idea: Jasper Udink ten Cate

Modernist Crudite

Let's get cheesy

MacGyver
Food solutions

Let's have lunch at the museum

ENJOY THE MOMENT..

TAKE YOUR TIME ON FASTFOOD

WE NEED YOU

TO JOIN THE SARDINES LIBERATION FRONT

think small.

PRACTISE
YOUR
CHOPS

From Creative Chef Postcards - © 2016 Jasper Udink ten Cate
and BIS Publishers - www.creativechef.nl - www.bispublishers.com

THE KNOCK OUT
HAMBURGER

DIFFICULT TIMES

PUZZLED COOKIES

Dinner
with the
kids?

КАЛАШНИКОВ СТЕЙК

KALASHNIKOV BEEF

SERVED WITH WODKA FROM THE BOTTLE